Maze Mouth

Maze Mouth

poems
by Brian Sonia-Wallace

~ 2023 ~

Maze Mouth
© Copyright 2023 Brian Sonia-Wallace
All rights reserved. No part of this book may be used or reproduced in any manner whatsoever without written permission from either the author or the publisher, except in the case of credited epigraphs or brief quotations embedded in articles or reviews.

Editor-in-chief
Eric Morago

Editor Emeritus
Michael Miller

Marketing Specialist
Ellen Webre

Proofreader
LeAnne Hunt

Front cover and interior art
Adrian Rodiguez

Author photo
Mandy Hoskinson

Book design
Michael Wada
Jeremy Ra

Moon Tide logo design
Abraham Gomez

Maze Mouth
is published by Moon Tide Press

Moon Tide Press
6709 Washington Ave. #9297 Whittier, CA 90608
www.moontidepress.com

FIRST EDITION

Printed in the United States of America

ISBN #978-1-957799-09-4

Contents

Part I – Before Language

Sonnet for Refuge	12
When Dad Died	13
Ars Poetica	16
Letter to a Minotaur from a 4th Grader	17
Death is Kinda a Dick	18
On Jacking Off to Dead Boys	19
The Typewriter Considers Running Away, *Again*	21
Migratory	22
Typewriter Confessional	23

Part II – Each of Us a Song

Out	26
The World is on Fire & I Have Something to Sell	27
Immolation	29
Best in Show	30
Renewal Ritual	31
The Star Map	32
You Keep Dating Latino Boys	33
Letter to a Minotaur from a 33-Year-Old	34
All My Desires Are a Size Too Small	35
The Oral Tradition	36

Part III – Care for the Living

Too Early to Celebrate?	38
Reverie with Penis and Adoring Dog	40
Here is a Gift You Can't Take With You	41
Care for the Living	42
Letter from the Minotaur to his Father	44
Heirloom	45
The Comfort Ghosts	46
After the Music	47
Can't You Find a Way	48
The Room You Just Left	49
About the Author	*51*
Acknowledgements	*52*

To imagine a language is to imagine a form of life.

— Cy Twombly

You shouldn't let poets lie to you.

— Björk

Part I

Before Language

Sonnet for Refuge

My family tree's full of corrupted forms.
English, my sweet mother's ancestral tongue,
my father's grandfather's salvation. Dead
now, that whole line, and me, queer, atheist,
childless, last of my name. Legacy's end.
No poem can escape its identity.
How Jewish, to fantasize extinction.
How gay. My people always leave. What if

I stay? In the absence of next-of-kin,
of God, commit myself to metaphor:
a family by any other name.
Fill poems with birds. Pale moons. Broken hearts.
Any eternal thing I think might last.
Beat forward, bearing armfuls of the past.

When Dad Died

1.

Family breaks, italicizes
into dialogue,
I miss him I miss him

two of us
at the table,
attempting a holiday —

    is that
    a family?

Mom heals, slowly.
Mind and body broken, booze-draggled,
teary drunk & showering only
as often as an injured person showers

    (how is that
    a mom?)

until, hungry for dog walks,
she rights herself on her cane
another date
with pain, that old, estranged lover
who moved in
when Dad died.

2.

When Dad died I got a fish.
When Dad died I started kickboxing.
When Dad died I broke up with everyone.
When Dad died I moved on.
When Dad died I taught.
When Dad died I could not think straight.
When Dad died I moved the car for street sweeping.
When Dad died I went to the desert.
When Dad died I had sex with strangers.
When Dad died I watered the new houseplants.
When Dad died I started to do
everything I'd ever do
for the rest of my life
after my dad died.

3.

A screeching devil of self-doubt
moved in, a few paperback prophets
and a podcast about setting boundaries,
communicating needs.

I give my mom Mother's Day.
She's needed. We open the good wine,
the wine he set aside.

We open the whiskey
I would have drunk with him
after she went to bed.

She stays up to drink the whiskey.
Near the end, she keeps saying
I'm so glad you're here.

4.

You have so much to live for,
emails a colleague of my dad's.

She laughs and laughs. *Isn't that funny?*
What does he think I'm going to do?
       (She keeps tracing the hole.)
I'm just complaining.

The setting sun complains
       golden across the street.
Jacarandas bother the sky.

I insist on a walk, and she grows animated
       inspecting the neighborhood,
hungry for new construction.

Ars Poetica

When a wound oozes, the doctors say, it expresses itself.

A dancing wound,
        a hollering wound,
                still sweating at midnight.

A wound is a High School hallway. All the trains are canceled
and no one here speaks English. English, the original wound.

When a wound twirls in, don't bury it.
When a wound woofs, howl back.

A wound is a wolf with a scent for family,
resenting the moon's wholeness.

The moon's wound was born before language.

Language:
        reaching,
                never whole.

The wolf, wolfs toward meaning.
Forget the doctors. Medicine isn't what we need.

Letter to a Minotaur from a 4th Grader

Dear Minotaur,

       Is it hard to live alone
in your labyrinth?

       Did you know I'm half
Jewish, so we're both half something?

       Red is my favorite color, too.
Would you attack me
       on sight if we met?

I would love you anyway,
       you know.

Death is Kinda a Dick

Death doesn't greet me
at the door to my parents house.
Death is rude. I'm offended,
but decide not to say anything,
to keep the peace.

We eat sushi, and Death's robe sleeve
keeps trailing in the soy sauce, wasabi
everywhere. I want to tell Death to knock it off,
but you can't tell Death to knock it off.
Death is definitely not listening.

I want to share the details of my day with Death,
my idle curiosities, but what's the point?
Death is terrible to bounce ideas off of.
Ideas just stick in Death. I try to tell Death
that my career is going great, but death just smiles
and never says a word.

Death never wants to have a glass of wine.
My mom and I drink enough for the three of us.
Toast my dad. *He was such a good man,* Death says.
Over and over again.

On Jacking Off to Dead Boys

As a teen, I practiced
lying to myself. My moonface

stretched and cratered. On the schoolyard,
boys trophy-hunted girl's kisses,

wet & alien. Midnight,
my dad'd finally go to bed, & I'd

search for rippling bellies & pits
like mine, fluffed, just another early 2000's

puka-shelled straight boy on a dirty couch
putting out for pay, looking straight

into the camera & lying,
it's my first time.

We wear our baseball caps low.
Don't give our real names.

I look the boy up. Learn he died at 25.
I've outlived them, the men who taught me desire.

Taught me to buy a puka-shell necklace.
Grow a goatee. Flee home. Any place that smelled like it.

I've slept on so many couches
my chest became a cushion.

I was raised to be anything
a camera asks. I can't stand to be around the same people

long enough for them to get to know me.
Secrets are my favorite part of myself.

Go ahead, call me two-faced.
I've got an infinite number of faces.

Friends keep giving me houseplants
like, *Here, you keep this alive.*

& I grieve my dad. I wish I could
tell him, *My wounds are working.*

Not every body has to be a grave.

The Typewriter Considers Running Away, *Again*

The trick is to not feel   al   one
          in your un   even spa   cing, sticky
keys, the odd   music that come   s out of yo   u,
     each time you move   to make a mark.

     The world is in   different,
this we   know. If you are leaping across
anything, it's you   rself.
          Don't slip   an identity on,

               carve it out. Michelangelo imagined
     David, already   in the rock. The Latin
gives us the w   ord "transgression," from
          "trans" (acr   oss) & "gradi" (go).

Who's still in   there, beg   ging
          to be let loos   e? What te   nder
machine, sw   eet monster, sa int?
          A dange   rous thin   g,

pa   ying attention. The ink sm   udges
          as it   dries. Your   letters run.
May as   well make frie   nds with your
          s   elf, before you're g   one.

Migratory

Tiny dogs tug at their leashes. They can't stop sniffing.
Addicts rub their arms at the intersection,

and the drag queens keep yassing and deathdropping.
A stranger messages you that he wants to be held

as he falls asleep. *Tuck me in?*
But, he says, *I don't sleep well with others.*

You'll have to leave right after. You leave
the country. Never get back to where you started.

Circle the dog park. Aren't we always
seeking something to return to?

The free little libraries in people's front yards
are delicate birdhouses, a flutter of migratory books.

The gym monitors the sauna for gay cruising, threatens
to terminate memberships. People carry on

exactly as they please. Sheriffs wake up a man sleeping on a bench
in the sun. Under your table, a small spider has made its home.

This could be home, you think, *this month*
or this city or this body. This poem.

*This poem was originally written for the City of West Hollywood's 2022 National Poetry Month celebration, and was meant to be read before City Council as part of my duties as Poet Laureate to create an annual poem celebrating the city. However, on submission, I was informed that it was "not the platform for this particular poem" due to "reference to addicts...[and to the] unhoused," but that I was free to submit it elsewhere. As a censored document, I invite the reader to consider what it means to celebrate a place, and why this piece about finding home could not find a home with the City.

Typewriter Confessional

No one asks, *what's this poem about?*
when you've written it on a typewriter
for them, after soliciting
their whole / life / story.

Not when you're set up
next to the
Rabbi / lip injection station / tarot reader

at the
wedding / makeup brand launch / all-company tech soiree

Instead of asking, your patrons cry
in front of their
spouses / employees / strangers.

They carry their shitty poem with its spelling mistakes
around the party, an excuse to talk to everyone
about their
dog / vacation / fear.

When you tell people you're a poet,
they ask, *is that your only job?*
Yes, you say. You work nights and weekends.

Your iPhone is full
of images of 5,000 first drafts (you counted)
you'll never edit. People you don't remember
bump into you years later and tell you they still have
their poem
on the fridge / in the bathroom / next to the bedside.

They reach out at new milestones
where you'll have no ability to backspace.
You're learning to edit in secret.
To make language strong enough
to hold you. You want to say, *this poem is about
how, even with people, I'm alone.*

But another stranger has brought you a glass
of bitter house red. They've remembered something
they want to tell *their* mother, something
they want you to say for them

only / better.

Part II
Each of Us a Song

Out

Boys stagger, honk
and moan across Robertson,
ripped booty shorts & painted talons,
mean as Mary Oliver's wild geese.
This ancestral flight path
of faggots: a nature poem.

Find me here, hungover, nesting
into my fifth cup of coffee.
When you have no wings,
only legs carry.
When you have no history,
you swallow the ghosts of strangers:

This family, this shimmy-flick, good gravel,
bones bones bones. Skeleton,
you have so much meat. Soft animal,
come in. Here is everything
you fled for so long. Come in.
You must be

                      lonely
           from all that
                  running.

The World is on Fire & I Have Something to Sell

I'd like to sell you the world. It's on fire.
But you should buy it — not because it's safe,
But because the economy —

(end of sentence). Have you been economical
with your words? With your worries? Have your worries
been eco-centric or ego-centric?

I would like to sell you an ego. A biome.
A life sentence. Take a look around. Lots to see.
Let me know if you have any questions.

Let me know if your questions have teeth.
Let me know if your teeth are chattering.
Or, if you do not have teeth, if you'd like some!

Actually — I'd like your teeth.
What would you like in exchange?
I only have the world. I don't carry exact change.

I carry exacting change. I carry messes
going back generations, gentlemen
callers with questions —

They check the teeth to make sure the horse
is healthy. You can tell a lot about a horse
from its teeth. How old it is. If it's broken to the bit.

Some horses have wolf teeth. Some are wind
suckers or crib biters. Check — does the horse
have ash in its mouth? Can it afford next month's rent?

The horse is sitting on a stack of photos.
It hasn't made the bed that broke its back.
The horse's mouth is a bed

for breaking. Hearts. Records. Bread.
Hooves no good with dirty dishes,
grimed through the open window—

Didn't you close it last night? No matter.
Throw it open now. Lasso the morning.
Breathe smoke. Wash your flank clean.

I have come to sell you a world on fire
& call it love. Love, the ash you carry
in your mouth. A bed for everything that's broken.

Immolation

When half your family dies & the other half
goes insane, you thread green lights
on summer nights toward hoodie weather,
replay future Thanksgivings at strange tables,

stuffing not your culture, you bread people
with simple butter, you dead people
ash-scattered with no funeral marker,
you run-away homecoming king

still chasing virgin dreams across continents
stale with Waffle House, Times Square
backdrop for make-up orgies, detention
in a lover's arms, he says, *boy, sit up straight,*

wipe that grin, inherit this wreckage
we call history, we call, again & again,
nothing to say just breathing into the phone
like, *fucker, I still can fog a windshield.*

I never know where I'm going.
It's out of fashion to write about loneliness,
but there, I said it, *I'm lonely.*
Parked in a dead man's car carrying a dead man's name

back to an empty house with stranger cum in my ass.
Who will re-attach my body to its language?
Who will fuck me when I live and, when I die,
tell them my final choice
was to be burned?

Best in Show

On the tail-end of a particularly Catholic
visit home to mom,
Steven inflated a balloon inside himself
& decided on his pup name:
Apollo, god of light.

Back in the city, he'd race to strip off
blue scrubs, firehose his insides
with a douche & fill
a Gatorade bottle with silicone lube.
Boys were waiting. Steven stayed loose.

Fists – if he was being honest – had gotten easy.
Last week, a man put his whole foot
in Steven's colon lining, soft earth on bare toes.
Apollo, the god, the dog, yelped
& whimpered, pawed the air,

head lancing back to lick
stars. Sometimes, at the nurse's station,
or on the volleyball court, Steven would reflexively
bark. In bed with his new husband (Dom, Daddy, Sir),
the boy growled tiredness & nuzzled his godhead in.

They slept that way until the sun rose.
Under daytime scrubs, Apollo wore a collar
with a dog tag in the shape of a bone.
What beast do you hide under your work shirt?
How wide does the god in you extend?

Maybe it isn't something for our mothers
to understand: This line of men, here for the ritual,
this hunger to be everyone's good boy.
To be the best boy.
To be.

Renewal Ritual

When'd you last tingle this cold? Unafraid,
unbirthed into the North Sea as it spat sunrise

& broke winter against our bodies,
pale & spotty 18-year-olds in bumfuck Scotland,

drunk on Tesco vodka, shivery,
belly aching for books, slurring distance

we huddled, a horny mass,
grubbed toward hot chocolate

steaming from the Christian Union's pop-up
tent under ruined fortress bluffs—

proffered with thin fingers like a sacrament,
like poison, like my mother.

Dawn.

I scratched
out my American tongue

to make space for milky builder's tea
& the salt sweet foreskins

of boys with strange vocabularies.
I made no plan to return.

A decade later, I dance
from a cryo chamber, -150° fahrenheit

with a reality star guru in West Hollywood,
arms tattooed for each transformation.

I wear the cold like an old lover's jacket.
You did so good for your first time,

he tells me, eyelashes frosted white.
You didn't even shiver.

The Star Map

An erasure poem from the Spanish language exhibition texts at the Getty Museum for the Codice Maya, the oldest surviving book from before the conquista *in North America, predicting the movements of the planet Venus for over 100 years. It is one of few books to survive the Spaniard's burning. Included in Spanish and in my translation.*

Casi todos	Almost all
sagrados	the sacred ones
perdieron	lose,
publicamente.	publicly.
Ahora	Now
aparesió	there appears
una falsificación	a falsification
trabajando de forma	working in
independiente,	an ancient,
antigua.	independent form.
Equipos de insectos	Teams of insects
utilizado	used
como pigmente rojo.	as red pigment.
Luz rasante	The raking light
muestra los daños	reveals the wounds
causado por	caused by
un calendario:	a calendar:
sacerdotes,	priests,
hechos catastróficos	catastrophic deeds,
signos de los días	sigils of the yellow
amarillos.	days.

You Keep Dating Latino Boys

If there's nopales in eggs
but a white person put them there,
are they still nopales?

If a white person says *te quiero*,
does desire mean consumption?

If a white person grows up speaking Spanish,
can they translate
the sound of brown bodies
falling?

Cade frontera, ficción, pesado y caro.
Puedes ganar mucha plata guardando una frontera.

The butcher throws out the parts
of the pig he can't sell.
The streets smell for miles
around the slaughterhouse.

¿Cierto que los latinos son más apasionados?

If a white person swallows
all their feelings,
all the time,
how much time
until they start to feel
full?

Letter to a Minotaur from a 33-Year-Old

Dear Minotaur,

Send help.

You get hungover too? After drinking all that
blood? I'm in a Motel 7 in Napa,
with a friend after wine tasting. Stomach
bloated with birria & Taco Bell & shrimp
from the drive, with everything growing
in this soil & fermenting in steel tub catacombs
kept at 55 degrees.

When I wake up, I idly catalog old lovers
& wonder if I could love any of them again.

Do you eat your prey indiscriminately,
or mourn each man who slides down your
gullet? Cataloging is a sort of mourning.
I am trying not to lose count.

In kindergarten, they used to make us stand
in line & count ourselves off, one, two, three,
before we could go inside.

Now I stand at the door & count one,
one,
one,
one,
one.

Until all of me is here
at the mouth of the maze.

All My Desires Are a Size Too Small

Slowing down
makes everything holy.
Terrifying.

Torn palm
fronds. Visiting
my mother.

I explain polyamory
to a doctor I'm dating
who has taken
off his jeans
to show me his
dick. It's a nice dick.

We kill time
talking
about our days.
He wants to know
my life plan.

I've never done
an honest day's work. I tell the truth
only at night. It makes me
look small. Because
I am.

I write
for skyscrapers.
My teeth, all
typewriters.
The words drip
down my chin
past their expiration date.

I will them
to be good.

When I was a knife, I longed
to do anything other than cut.

The Oral Tradition

Your fetish is worship.
Believing a body can be whole
enough to be holy.

The big-dicked Texan is a treasure trove
of conspiracy theories. Pretty sure it's the meth.
He's starting to get familiar

& you want to tell him, *shhh — no — I'm using you
exclusively for your dick*. Even with a dick like that,
he can scarcely hide his despair.

You've been stockpiling weddings
& funerals. Smashing lovers to scavenge
for parts, nibbling mouthfuls of long-dead gods.

Texas wants to watch *Ancient Aliens* on YouTube.
You recognize the story about men from the sky
as a literal interpretation of a Sumerian origin story:

For knowledge of sex, Innana gives up
a symbol of her power at each of seven gates
of the underworld, until she arrives naked.

I wish you'd shut up, you want to say
to Texas, *so I can write you a better
mythology. I already know how this one*

ends.

Part III
Care for the Living

Too Early to Celebrate?
a collaborative poem using words and memories contributed by West Hollywood residents

Won't you walk with me
my glam aunts, my ferocious uncles,
my frankest friends — my chosen family.
Look at all we have lost.
All that survives.
We are a house
built
on bones. We are dancing.
Dancing on bones.

You, dear, never stopped
being a proud march, a palm
frond in ragged wind —
yes, you curled up
in last winter's hush.
This city threads us
lonely
a plastic oasis of skin
sweaty with starlight.

But now it's time for
gogo boots & guitar strings,
rooftop pools & history
between your lips
like a cold margarita
while the hot asphalt
dances.
Each of us a song:
equal parts party and protest.

The sunset strip
echoes, jacarandas bloom bright
after barren months.
Our streets symphony again
wild beyond gardens,
blaze honey
disco
French horns
& orange sherbet glow.

Reverie with Penis and Adoring Dog

In the editorial fashion photo, a child looks out the window,
away from the model, her mother—presumably—who

fixes us, from an armchair, with a sultry gaze. It's easy
to read the child as the model's younger self, looking

away, or perhaps looking ahead, dreaming of one day
being so glamorous. This photo is on my friend's vision board.

He's the son of a porn star, and over the model's legs
he's glued a huge penis. *A mer-penis!* he calls it,

like a mermaid but with a phallus instead of a tail.
I'm so distracted by the dick I don't notice until much later

that there's a third figure in the photograph: a golden retriever,
looking lovingly up at the model. If the child is a younger self,

could the dog be that as well? Or an older self?
In the rain forests of Ecuador, the Shuar say that sloths

are very old people who have returned to the forest
and climbed into the trees to rest. Perhaps one day,

the model will be as happy, looking at us, as the dog is,
gazing at her. Perhaps one day, I'll be happy.

We'll all be dogs, chasing lifeless balls with all the urgency
of our imaginations. And then, we'll be dead. A little girl

will look out the window. A photograph will remain.
Someone's son will scrapbook a huge cock over our legs

and say: *Yes.*
This is my dream.

Here is a Gift You Can't Take With You

Lover, I aim to haunt you
with my joy. When you pick me up
from the airport, give you the squirm

of my enthusiasm & ask,
will you feed this?
I let you go a long time ago.

My sorrow is small-stomached, but happiness
is always hungry. Prepare me a feast of lost years & I
will set the table. You worry like it's your religion, but

I hear you're feeding parts of yourself
I never could, and my world expands through
emulation — the opposite of envy.

I am flying. I am flying to you.
You are far away. Full of gifts
I do not covet. From seeds we learn:

To love something
is to leave it long enough
to grow.

Care for the Living

I emerge from the purple-lit bedroom.
We've been gangbanging yet *another* Steven.
Devon hands me a betta fish in a sealed cup,
scales fluorescent blue, a jar of fish food
and a tank like a flower vase.

I got you a fish! he says.

It's his place. I've gotten comfortable.
Today, he came quick and left
for the pharmacy before it closed.
Not before grabbing his neighbor,
out walking three small yorkies,
and sending him in.

There's an awkward, balls-deep pause.
Then the neighbor, tattooed and silver-haired,
ties his dogs to the door handle, drops his jeans,
and joins in. I grin at him. We trade
Instagram handles.

Only in West Hollywood.

The fish circles with its mouth
open. Every time I'm in Devon's house,
new scales flash from tanks around the walls.
He keeps saying he's going to move.
Gets rid of more furniture. Stays
up all night. *Meth?* I think, but don't ask.
He shows me his scars. Reckless driving tickets.
Complains of back pain. Never moves away.
I warn myself not to get attached.
We walk the block with a cigarette, and his bulldog
attacks a traffic cone.

They never stop building, in this neighborhood.

When Steven arrived, hole hungry, he'd dosed so much G,
he could barely walk. I have to explain the new fish
to my roommate. Name him Charlemagne.
Drop by the pet store for the first time since I was a kid
to pick up water purifier, ten drops and everything
that gushes out of the taps
becomes a suitable home for life.

Letter from the Minotaur to his Father

Dad	Dad	Dad	Dad				
Dad	Dad	Dad	Dad				
	Dad	Dad	Dad	Dad			
	Dad	Dad	Dad	Red			
		Red	Dad	Dad	Dad		
		Dad	Dad	Dad	Dad		
			Dad	Dad	Dad	Dad	
			Dad	Dad	Rad	Dad	
				Red	Red	Red	Red
				Red	Red	Red	Red
					Dad	Dad	Dad	Dad
					Dead	Dead	Dead	Dead

Heirloom

Dad always grew tomatoes.
They were his pride and joy.
So when the lady outside Home Depot
offered me the box and said,
Do you have a garden?
I didn't say no, though I should have.
I said, *We have a theatre…*
and somehow that was just as good.

It grows like a weed in Hollywood
in the cracks between Film and Industry.
It was a grease monkey's garage,
then a shooting range,
but only now
can we call the people who run it clowns.
We put the tomatoes out
on the air conditioning supply unit
to try to add some poetry to that phrase.

Today is tomatoes in the parking lot.
Tomorrow is white roof, filtered water, solar
panels, cycle racks, urban garden, green
building, public plaza, artist's village —
to build a cultural heritage for the city
I once heard described as *Hell's Parking Lot,*
tomato by tomato,
because nobody dreams as hard as poets
and nobody works as hard as clowns.

The Comfort Ghosts

They are all here,
generations of queers,
elders with crooked hands
like trees. I shake myself
at the giant's trunk
to see the grove glisten.
Invisible branches
shimmer suddenly in the light.

If only the roots could see the budding sky.

If only I could garden my history so deep.

Strength. Pride.
To be burned, emptied.
To stand tall, anyway, play host
to new shoots, fresh green,
a forest with a single
root system.

Whatever they say of us, let them say,

we didn't do this alone.

After the Music

Praise the Zoom call.
You're on mute, love!
Can't hear you —
(secretly) Praise (the bad) connection.

Praise our home offices, our home schools,
our home gyms, our closed bars, our kitchen dances,
our cooking fails, our odd jobs. Our rented
U-Hauls. Our promises to stay.

In a workshop (online, duh), my friend Dorsay,
a resplendent seventy-five, crowned in Diana Ross curls,
shares her poem: butterflies, a lover's caress
and then — *Why should I not want to just die?*

She seeded concerts across the city for decades.
Now, it's impossible to sing together. Everyone is slightly
out of time. What happens after the music?
We gape and stammer, but Dorsay —

she booms laughter, claps her hands.
We're here aren't we? However we gather,
it's a party. Our face parade, through lag and crash, and latency,
logging on against erasure. *I'll be there*

next week, writes Dorsay. A late-night promise.
The next morning, bougainvillea shocks pink
across the sidewalk. I leave the Russian bakery
with a loaf of black Borodinsky rye.

Praise the long walk, with no end. The right now.
Our newly fragiled bodies.
That awkward, grateful way we hold each other
at any distance.

Can't You Find a Way

>*You've been sleeping for miles / so what did you see?*
>— from "Empire Line," by The National

A sliver of water, hemmed in concrete,
guides me & my aching calves
to the Pacific, where families defy bedtimes,

dangle lures of laughter off a bridge,
catch polluted fish. We are from
the dream factory.

In the hands of the mountains (at the water's
mouth) (under summer's cruel boot-heel)
the city is taking off its clothes.

I'm only an adolescent, so I don't know
what to do with a naked city. I'm working up the guts
to run away.

Goodbye dogs
with thunderous
jowls, goodbye

late-night pancakes,
goodbye screaming
skinny dips, beach bonfires,

wet & smoggy
kisses,
goodbye.

When all else is gone, I want to remember
myself like this: naked as a whole city,
jumping into the gray

Pacific.

The Room You Just Left

Move the car for street sweeping.
The workout rotation: legs, chest, back.
Breathe books & drink it black &
every haircut is a complete reinvention—

the cycle of coffee
with mom, crying with mom—
every time you put on your shoes,
you will never re-enter the room you just left.

My old lover tells me I am building a ritual.
I see him infrequently. I see him again.
My mom tells me she is useless.
I am stern: *Stop being mean to my mom.*

The pit of my stomach tells me
everything I want to hear. It sings,
the thinnest spiderweb, a wail of egrets,
white-streaked against the sky.

Without warning, Dad is dead.
Every meal, every bike ride, a reminder.
The hole doesn't close, Mom says,
you just have to embroider around the edges.

Like beauty is the pain we attend to.
Like the only way to keep living

                is to practice.

About the Author

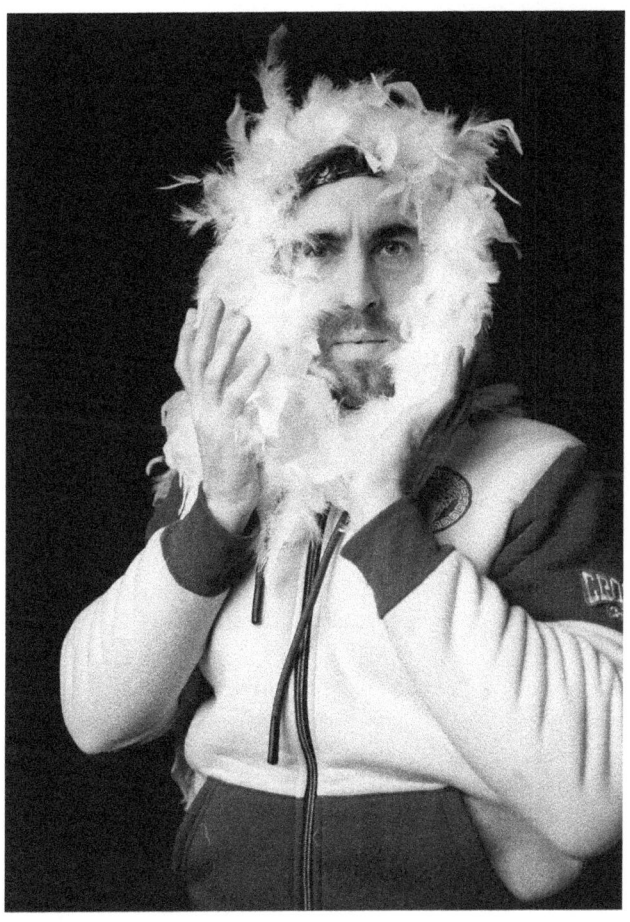

Brian Sonia-Wallace is the 4th Poet Laureate of the City of West Hollywood, an Academy of American Poets Laureate Fellow for LGBTQ+ literary activism, and the author of *The Poetry of Strangers: What I Learned Traveling America with a Typewriter*. His book chronicles long-term project RENT Poet, which invites the public to share their stories in exchange for poems about them, written in real-time on a vintage typewriter. Brian has received odd writer's residencies from Amtrak and the Mall of America, and teaches through the UCLA Extension Writers' Program. More at briansoniawallace.com.

Acknowledgements

I am grateful to the editors of the following publications and projects in which these poems previously appeared, sometimes in a slightly different form or with a different title, and for the many collaborators who have had a hand in shaping each.

The City of West Hollywood, National Poetry Month: "Migratory" and "Too Early to Celebrate?"

The Academy of American Poets' *Poets.org*: "The Comfort Ghosts," "Heirloom" and "Too Early to Celebrate?"

Choral works with composer Saunder Choi for gay choirs across America: "The Comfort Ghosts" (as "Generations") and "Too Early to Celebrate?" (as "Our Streets a Symphony").

WeHoVille: "Too Early to Celebrate?"

Healthy Environments Across Generations Conference, New York Academy of Medicine: "Heirloom."

Margin Releases: Typewritten Tales of Transgression: "The Typewriter Considers Running Away, t."

The Los Angeles Press, Volume 6: "Here is a Gift You Can't Take With You" and "Renewal Ritual."

The Los Angeles Press, Volume 7: "Sonnet for Refuge."

14 Poems (UK): "Immolation."

Queer Quarterly, Volume 3: "Out."

Thanks to members of my community for their advice, support, and feedback in helping to bring these poems into the world: Linda Ravenswood, Kelly Grace Thomas, Melanie Zoe Weinstein, Carla Sameth, Bryn Wickerd, and Brooking Gatewood. Thanks to Nate Lovell, Tony Velovski, and The Mic @ Micky's team for our space and community where many of these poems lived out loud for the first time.

Thanks to Eric Morago and Moon Tide Press for giving these poems a home, and Jeremy Ra for bringing me into the family. And thanks to the manuscript critique group for their feedback: Kristen Baum, Nicelle Davis, Patti Scruggs, Rosie Freed, Kathleen Goldman, Terri Niccum, P.K., Shelly Holder, and Elaine Mintzer.

Thanks to Mike Che and the City of West Hollywood for allowing me to serve as their poet laureate, and to the Academy of American Poets Laureate Fellowship for the time and space to write.

Also Available from Moon Tide Press

Another Way of Loving Death, Jeremy Ra (2023)
Tangled by Blood, Rebecca Evans (2023)
Kissing the Wound, J.D. Isip (2023)
Feed It to the River, Terhi K. Cherry (2022)
Beat Not Beat: An Anthology of California Poets Screwing on the Beat and Post-Beat Tradition (2022)
When There Are Nine: Poems Celebrating the Life an Achievements of Ruth Bader Ginsburg (2022)
The Knife Thrower's Daughter, Terri Niccum (2022)
2 Revere Place, Aruni Wijesinghe (2022)
Here Go the Knives, Kelsey Bryan-Zwick (2022)
Trumpets in the Sky, Jerry Garcia (2022)
Threnody, Donna Hilbert (2022)
A Burning Lake of Paper Suns, Ellen Webre (2021)
Instructions for an Animal Body, Kelly Gray (2021)
Head *V* Heart: New & Selected Poems, Rob Sturma (2021)
Sh!t Men Say to Me: A Poetry Anthology in Response to Toxic Masculinity (2021)
Flower Grand First, Gustavo Hernandez (2021)
Everything is Radiant Between the Hates, Rich Ferguson (2020)
When the Pain Starts: Poetry as Sequential Art, Alan Passman (2020)
This Place Could Be Haunted If I Didn't Believe in Love, Lincoln McElwee (2020)
Impossible Thirst, Kathryn de Lancellotti (2020)
Lullabies for End Times, Jennifer Bradpiece (2020)
Crabgrass World, Robin Axworthy (2020)
Contortionist Tongue, Dania Ayah Alkhouli (2020)
The only thing that makes sense is to grow, Scott Ferry (2020)
Dead Letter Box, Terri Niccum (2019)
Tea and Subtitles: Selected Poems 1999-2019, Michael Miller (2019)
At the Table of the Unknown, Alexandra Umlas (2019)
The Book of Rabbits, Vince Trimboli (2019)
Everything I Write Is a Love Song to the World, David McIntire (2019)
Letters to the Leader, HanaLena Fennel (2019)
Darwin's Garden, Lee Rossi (2019)
Dark Ink: A Poetry Anthology Inspired by Horror (2018)
Drop and Dazzle, Peggy Dobreer (2018)
Junkie Wife, Alexis Rhone Fancher (2018)
The Moon, My Lover, My Mother, & the Dog, Daniel McGinn (2018)
Lullaby of Teeth: An Anthology of Southern California Poetry (2017)

Angels in Seven, Michael Miller (2016)
A Likely Story, Robbi Nester (2014)
Embers on the Stairs, Ruth Bavetta (2014)
The Green of Sunset, John Brantingham (2013)
The Savagery of Bone, Timothy Matthew Perez (2013)
The Silence of Doorways, Sharon Venezio (2013)
Cosmos: An Anthology of Southern California Poetry (2012)
Straws and Shadows, Irena Praitis (2012)
In the Lake of Your Bones, Peggy Dobreer (2012)
I Was Building Up to Something, Susan Davis (2011)
Hopeless Cases, Michael Kramer (2011)
One World, Gail Newman (2011)
What We Ache For, Eric Morago (2010)
Now and Then, Lee Mallory (2009)
Pop Art: An Anthology of Southern California Poetry (2009)
In the Heaven of Never Before, Carine Topal (2008)
A Wild Region, Kate Buckley (2008)
Carving in Bone: An Anthology of Orange County Poetry (2007)
Kindness from a Dark God, Ben Trigg (2007)
A Thin Strand of Lights, Ricki Mandeville (2006)
Sleepyhead Assassins, Mindy Nettifee (2006)
Tide Pools: An Anthology of Orange County Poetry (2006)
Lost American Nights: Lyrics & Poems, Michael Ubaldini (2006)

Patrons

Moon Tide Press would like to thank the following people for their support in helping publish the finest poetry from the Southern California region. To sign up as a patron, visit www.moontidepress.com or send an email to publisher@moontidepress.com.

Anonymous
Robin Axworthy
Conner Brenner
Nicole Connolly
Bill Cushing
Susan Davis
Kristen Baum DeBeasi
Peggy Dobreer
Kate Gale
Dennis Gowans
Alexis Rhone Fancher
HanaLena Fennel
Half Off Books & Brad T. Cox
Donna Hilbert
Jim & Vicky Hoggatt
Michael Kramer
Ron Koertge & Bianca Richards
Gary Jacobelly
Ray & Christi Lacoste
Jeffery Lewis
Zachary & Tammy Locklin
Lincoln McElwee
David McIntire
José Enrique Medina
Michael Miller & Rachanee Srisavasdi
Michelle & Robert Miller
Ronny & Richard Morago
Terri Niccum
Andrew November
Jeremy Ra
Luke & Mia Salazar
Jennifer Smith
Roger Sponder
Andrew Turner
Rex Wilder
Mariano Zaro
Wes Bryan Zwick

www.ingramcontent.com/pod-product-compliance
Lightning Source LLC
Chambersburg PA
CBHW021000090426
42736CB00010B/1405